ANIMAL RIVALS

Lion
VS.
Tiger

Isabel Thomas

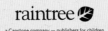

a Capstone company — publishers for children

Raintree is an imprint of Capstone Global Library Limited, a company incorporated in England and Wales having its registered office at 264 Banbury Road, Oxford, OX2 7DY – Registered company number: 6695582

www.raintree.co.uk
myorders@raintree.co.uk

Edited by Penny McLoughlin
Designed by Steve Mead
Picture research by Svetlana Zhurkin
Production by Katy LaVigne
Printed and bound in China

ISBN 978 1 474 74452 2
21 20 19 18 17
10 9 8 7 6 5 4 3 2 1

British Library Cataloguing in Publication Data
A full catalogue record for this book is available from the British Library.

Acknowledgements
We would like to thank the following for permission to reproduce photographs: Getty Images: Nature Picture Library/Andy Parkinson, 19, 22 (bottom right), Nature Picture Library/Anup Shah, 8, 22 (top right, bottom left); Minden Pictures: Elliott Neep, 17; Newscom: Splash News/Solent News, 18, VWPics/Gerard Lacz, 9, 22 (middle left); Shutterstock: apple2499, 20, BBA Photography, back cover (right), 5, crazycolors, back cover (left), 16, davemhuntphotography, cover (left), e2dan, 14, Eric Isselee, 21, FCG, 12, Gerrit_de_Vries, 6, Glass and Nature, 13, Graeme Shannon, 10, 22 (top left), Martin Prochazkacz, 7, nale (silhouette), 6, 7, pashabo (texture), cover and throughout, PhotocechCZ, 11, Rostislav Stach, 4, 22 (middle right), Sharon Morris, cover (right), shin, 15

Every effort has been made to contact copyright holders of material reproduced in this book. Any omissions will be rectified in subsequent printings if notice is given to the publisher.

All the Internet addresses (URLs) given in this book were valid at the time of going to press. However, due to the dynamic nature of the Internet, some addresses may have changed, or sites may have changed or ceased to exist since publication. While the author and publisher regret any inconvenience this may cause readers, no responsibility for any such changes can be accepted by either the author or the publisher.

Some words are shown in bold, **like this**.
You can find them in the glossary on page 22.

Contents

Meet the animals

What has a **shaggy** mane and a loud roar?

It's the **African lion**.

What has striped fur and a long tail?

It's the
Bengal
tiger.

Would a lion or a tiger win in a fight?
Let's find out!

Size and strength

A lion has powerful shoulder **muscles** for grabbing its prey. A male lion's mane makes him look bigger than he really is.

This is how tall a lion is next to a human.

This is how tall a tiger is next to a human.

A tiger weighs as much as 50 pet cats! It uses its huge body to knock down animals up to twice its size.

Speed

A lion can only **sprint** for a short time. It will give up if its prey gets ahead. Buffalos are **massive** but slow. They are easier to catch than speedy gazelles.

A tiger is a little faster than a lion. But it also cannot run for long. Strong leg **muscles** make a tiger good at jumping and climbing.

Coats

A lion needs to hide to get close to its prey before it attacks. Its sandy-coloured coat **blends** in perfectly with the pale African grass.

The bright orange coat of a tiger may look easy to spot. But its prey can't see bright colours. The stripes make it harder to see.

Survival skills

Lions are often called lazy. They rest between meals to save energy. A lion mostly hunts at night, when it's not as hot.

A tiger may have to walk a long way to find food. Tough pads protect its paws from cuts and scratches. It loves to cool off by taking a swim.

Super senses

A lion has fantastic eyesight. It can spot prey far across the African plains. A lion can see six times better than a human in the dark.

A tiger can twist its ears to hear all around. A tiger's whiskers come in handy at night. They feel tiny air movements that show something is moving nearby.

Deadly weapons

A lion's bite is 30 times stronger than the bite of a pet cat. With its strong jaw and razor-sharp teeth, a lion can kill with a single bite.

paw

claw

A tiger has super-sharp hooked claws that help it catch its prey. When the tiger isn't using them, it hides them in its paws, like a pet cat.

Fighting skills

A male lion will fight to scare off other males or stop other animals from stealing food. Male lions will often fight to the death.

Lions live in groups, but tigers live alone.
A tiger that can't hunt will starve, so it tries
to avoid risky fights. Male tigers **wrestle** to
scare the weaker one away.

Who wins?

What would happen if a lion faced a tiger? The animals would snarl and roar. They would **wrestle** and try to bite each other.

But who would win?

	Lion	Tiger
Size	8	8
Strength	9	8
Speed	6	7
Energy	7	8
Coats	7	9
Senses	9	9
Claws	7	7
Jaws	10	8
Hunting skills	7	8
Fighting skills	7	8
TOTAL	**80/100**	79/100

LION
WINS!

Picture glossary

blend fit in well with the things around it

massive very big

muscle a part of the body that causes movement

shaggy thick and untidy

sprint run fast for a short distance

wrestle fight by trying to flip the enemy over or hold them down on the ground

Find out more

Books

Big Cats (Explorers), Claire Llewellyn (Kingfisher, 2016)

Lions (Animal Lives), Sally Morgan (QED Publishing, 2014)

Lions Are Awesome! (Awesome African Animals!), Lisa J. Amstutz (Raintree, 2015)

Websites

www.learninggamesforkids.com/animal-games-big-cats.html
Play games and watch videos about your favourite big cats.

www.ngkids.co.uk/animals/10-tiger-facts
Find ten fierce facts about tigers.

www.sciencekids.co.nz/sciencefacts/animals/tiger.html
Learn more about tigers and their cubs on this website.

Index